THE TROJAN WAR

A legendary conflict in Ancient Greece

Written by Benoît-J. Pédretti
In collaboration with Damien Glad
Translated by Jessica Foster

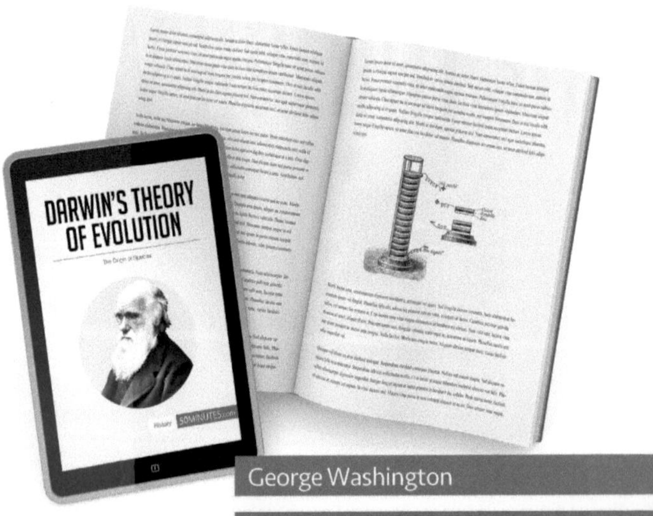

THE TROJAN WAR

KEY INFORMATION

- **When:** mid-13th century BC, or early 12th century BC.
- **Where:** in Greece and Asia Minor.
- **Context:** during a diplomatic mission to Greece, Paris, the son of the king of Troy, kidnapped Helen, the queen of Sparta. The Greek cities thus sent their armies to Troy in order to rescue the young woman. According to Homer, a ten-year war ensued.
- **Key protagonists:**
  - Helen, queen of Sparta
  - Menelaus, king of Sparta, Helen's husband and Agamemnon's brother
  - Agamemnon, king of Mycenae, Menelaus's brother
  - Achilles, king of the Myrmidons
  - Patroclus, Achilles' friend and cousin
  - Odysseus, king of Ithaca
  - Priam, king of Troy
  - Hector and Paris, princes of Troy.
- **Outcome:** after many twists, the Trojan War ended in the capture and destruction of the city by the Achaeans (the name given to the Greeks at the time). The brave soldiers, both Achaeans and Trojans, fell one by one during battle. Achilles himself, who was a demigod, died from an arrow shot into his heel. Those who survived scattered across the Mediterranean and founded illustrious cities. This was notably the case for Aeneas, whose descendent Romulus founded the city of Rome.

INTRODUCTION

The Trojan War, the epic saga of Greek Antiquity, originated from the struggle between men and the gods. Aphrodite had promised Paris the love of the world's most beautiful woman. With her support, he kidnapped Helen, whom he believed to be the most stunning woman in the world, and fled with her to Troy.

Menelaus, who wanted his wife back, called upon his brother Agamemnon, king of Mycenae, the most powerful Greek city at the time. He united armies from every city behind him and launched the largest military campaign ever led by the Greeks against Troy. The formidable armada landed on the Trojan shores. The attack was repelled several times, as Hector organised a fierce resistance behind the city's high walls, which were reputed to be impenetrable. With the decisive help of Achilles and the Myrmidons, after many epic battles and the famous ruse of the Trojan horse, the city was finally captured and pillaged. Helen was taken back to Sparta. Many heroes, including Achilles, Hector and Paris, died during the battle, but their legendary adventures have lived on through the centuries.

CONTEXT

HELEN'S MARRIAGE AND TYNDAREUS'S PROMISE

When Helen, the daughter of Tyndareus, king of Sparta, came of age, her legendary beauty attracted many suitors. All the Achaean kings and war leaders sought her hand. Tyndareus did not want to anger these powerful kings, as a blunder on his part could revive internal disputes between the cities. Odysseus, the king of Ithaca, suggested a way to escape this predicament, undoubtedly in the hope of impressing the father to win his daughter. Following his advice, a horse was sacrificed and its skin thrown on the ground. All of Helen's suitors were then invited to gather around it. This was a symbolic gesture: they had to promise to form a coalition alliance which would fight anyone who tried to take Helen from her new husband. This ingenious promise enabled Tyndareus to be sure that none of them would disrupt the stability in Greece after Helen was married.

According to some sources, Helen herself chose the one she loved the most, Menelaus. However, it is more likely that her father chose him personally, as Menelaus was the richest of her suitors. Tyndareus entrusted him with his throne at the same time as his daughter.

THE GOLDEN APPLE OF DISCORD

The *Cypria*, an epic poem whose events take place before those of the *Iliad*, tells us that Eris, the goddess of strife and discord, wanted to get revenge for having not been invited to the wedding of Peleus and Thetis on Mount Olympus. To do this, she decided to throw a golden apple, bearing the inscription "To the fairest", into the middle of the banquet, without stating whom it was really for. All the goddesses tried to claim it, but only Hera, the wife of Zeus, Athena, the goddess of war, and Aphrodite, the goddess of love, ended up competing over it. An external judge was required to make the final decision: they chose a mere mortal. The three goddesses were taken to Mount Ida, near Troy, where a young shepherd was asked to decide between them. In exchange for his favourable decision, Hera promised him power over mortals, Athena promised him victory in battle and Aphrodite promised him the love of the world's most beautiful woman. The shepherd, who was none other than Paris, awarded the golden apple to Aphrodite, and thus gained the goddess's protection and the love she had promised him. Nobody knew that he was the son of the king of Troy. On the other hand, he believed that the most beautiful woman in the world was the king of Sparta's new bride, Helen.

The Judgement of Paris, painting by Rubens, 1632-1635

HELEN'S KIDNAPPING

During a previous war, the king of Salamis, Telamon, had kidnapped Hesione, the sister of Priam, king of Troy. Once the tensions between Troy and Greece had subsided, Priam sent a diplomatic peace mission to cities in Greece, led by his two sons, Hector, the oldest, and Paris, the youngest. Some versions of the story suggest that the objective of this mission was to demand Hesione's return.

Whatever the exact aim was, the delegation was warmly welcomed by all the Achaean cities. In Sparta, the new king, Menelaus, received them in splendour. However, he was then called to his dying grandfather's bedside in Crete. Subsequently, Paris fell in love with Queen Helen. Consenting and in love or, according to other sources, kidnapped by force, Helen boarded the fleet that was taking the Trojans back to Asia Minor. She was welcomed by Priam, and was married to Paris immediately.

The Abduction of Helen, painting by Guido Reni, 1626-1629.

Although the Trojans considered that Helen's kidnapping was proof of Aphrodite's approval, the Achaeans respected the promise made to Tyndareus and formed a coalition against a common foreign enemy, Helen's kidnapper.

The Trojan War had been declared.

BIOGRAPHIES OF THE KEY PROTAGONISTS

THE ACHAEANS

Queen Helen of Sparta

Helen was the daughter of King Tyndareus of Sparta and his wife Leda. However, many epics attribute a more illustrious father to her: Zeus. Incomparably beautiful, she had already been kidnapped a few years earlier by Theseus, the king of Athens, then saved by her brothers, the twins Castor and Pollux.

Her father decided to have her married to Menelaus, to whom he also handed over his throne: Helen thus became the queen of Sparta. When she was kidnapped by Paris, she was at the origin of the most famous epic saga of Antiquity: the Trojan War. Following the fall of Troy and the death of her kidnapper, she returned to her first husband. Menelaus, who wanted revenge for the humiliation he had suffered, initially planned to kill her. However, he fell in love with her once again and eventually decided to take her back with him. Their return journey across the Mediterranean lasted eight years.

When Menelaus died, the Spartans chased Helen out, and she was forced to flee to Rhodes. Held responsible for the death of the city's king during the assault on Troy, she was murdered in her bathtub by Queen Polyxo's handmaidens. Her body was then hung from a tree and exposed to the vengeful public.

She was worshipped in Sparta for centuries, and is the heroine whose legendary and breathtaking beauty has been recounted to us by mythology.

King Menelaus of Sparta, Helen's husband and Agamemnon's brother

Menelaus was the youngest son of Atreus, king of Mycenae, and his wife, Aerope. Raised with his older brother Agamemnon and their sister Anaxibia, he was exiled as a child by his cousin Aegisthus. As an adult, he helped his brother to reclaim the Mycenaean throne. Despite Helen's many suitors, he was the one who won the hand of Tyndareus's daughter, as well as the throne of Sparta. Two children were born from this marriage: Hermione and Nicostratus.

Occupied in Crete during the Trojan mission to Sparta, he could do nothing to prevent his wife's kidnapping. Once he had been informed of his misfortune, he went to Agamemnon to ask for his support and for the help of the Achaeans who had been part of the promise. He then led a mission alongside Odysseus and went to Troy to get his wife back. Homer recounts how, during the assault on the city, he saw Paris in the fray and went to fight him. Paris withdrew at the last minute, which saved his life on that occasion. Unable to satisfy his thirst for vengeance, Menelaus became even more aggressive. A seasoned fighter, he was one of the men who entered Troy inside the famous Trojan horse. He found his wife and brought her back to Sparta, after filling his ship's hold with gold. He spent the rest of his life peacefully in Sparta.

Described in texts as feisty and full of bravado, with a mop of blond hair, he was considered to be the most slighted of the Greeks, but, in the end, would remain a secondary protagonist in the Trojan War.

Agamemnon, king of Mycenae, Menelaus's brother

Agamemnon was the eldest son of Atreus, king of Mycenae. He married Clytemnestra, the other daughter of the king of Sparta, with whom he would have four children: Chrysothemis, Electra, Iphigenia and Orestes. When his father died and Aegisthus was overthrown, Agamemnon came to the throne in Mycenae, which was then the most powerful city in Greece. Following Helen's kidnapping, he was chosen by the Achaeans to lead the campaign against Troy. He was the head of the army throughout the war.

Once the fighting was finished, he returned to Mycenae, where he was assassinated by Aegisthus, who had seduced his wife. Pindar (Ancient Greek poet, 518-438 BC) even goes as far as to state that it was most likely Clytemnestra herself who killed him.

Achilles, king of the Myrmidons

Achilles was the son of Peleus, king of the Myrmidons, and the goddess Thetis. He was a demigod who is thought of as the true hero of the Trojan War. Raised in Larissa by his mother, he was able to choose his destiny: to have a short life and be crowned in glory, to the extent that his name would be remembered centuries after his death; or to have a long, peaceful but totally anonymous life. Achilles chose glory.

While he was absent from the Trojan War for a long time, Odysseus finally convinced him to support the Achaean army. He led his elite warriors, the Myrmidons, and gave the Greeks a decisive advantage until he pulled out of the war following a dispute with Agamemnon. The death of his friend Patroclus would drive him back to the battlefield, to avenge him. There he faced Hector, Priam's son, whom he killed before being shot in the heel by Paris with a fatal arrow.

DID YOU KNOW?

We use the term 'Achilles' heel' to describe a person's weak spot. The most popular legend states, in fact, that Thetis submerged her newborn son in the waters of the River Styx, with the aim of making him immortal. Her son's body thus became invincible, as though it were covered by invisible and impenetrable armour. However, it was impossible to immerse him completely: as she submerged him headfirst, she had to hold him firmly by his heel, which thus became the only part of his body that could not benefit from this magical protection. Some iconographic representations depict his death with an arrow in his lower thigh, but most literary sources agree that 'heel' is a more appropriate translation.

Patroclus, Achilles' friend and cousin

Patroclus, son of Menoetius, was a close friend and cousin of Achilles, whom he accompanied to Troy as both his horseman and messenger. It should be noted that Homer is the only one who omits all mention of a romantic relationship between Patroclus and Achilles.

During the war, when Achilles returned from battle to his tent, Patroclus borrowed his weaponry and led to Myrmidons to the battlefield. He was killed during a one-on-one combat with Hector, and his body was taken back to Achilles. Driven mad by grief, Achilles took up arms and avenged his friend by killing Hector. Patroclus's body was cremated on a gigantic pyre, and a grand funeral was organised in his honour.

Odysseus, king of Ithaca

Son of Laertes and Anticlea, Odysseus was the king of Ithaca and several surrounding islands. He married Penelope, the daughter of Icarius and Periboea. Together they had a son, Telemachus.

Odysseus was present from the beginning of the Trojan War. On the Achaeans' side, he gave the impression of a wise, shrewd king. He was also in charge of all the diplomatic missions and negotiations, both before and during the war. He is also said to be the instigator of the Trojan horse ploy.

Moreover, he is the hero of the *Odyssey*, Homer's other epic, which recounts how, on his way back from the Trojan War, Odysseus wandered the Ionian Sea in a long maritime voyage, during which he encountered the magician Circe and the cyclops Polyphemus. As he had been gone for 20 years, he was presumed dead in Ithaca, where his wife Penelope was putting off all the claimants to the throne who wanted to marry her. Having promised that she would choose her next husband once her tapestry was finished, she made sure that every evening she undid the work she had done during the day. When Odysseus returned to Ithaca, he recovered his throne and his family. According to Homer, the rest of his life was peaceful.

THE TROJANS

King Priam of Troy

Priam, son of Laomedon and Strymo, was the king of Troy when the war broke out. He was married to Hecuba and was the father of many children, including the princes of Troy, Hector and Paris. Described by Homer as a wise, just and righteous king, he sent his sons on a diplomatic mission to the cities of Greece, including Sparta. During the war, he lost his eldest son, Hector, who was killed by Achilles. Devastated, and hoping to recover his son's body to give him the customary funeral honours, he went to the Achaean camp, risking his life, to beg Achilles to give him his son's body, which he obtained. During the capture of Troy, he was killed in his palace by Neoptolemus, the son of Achilles.

Hector, prince of Troy

Hector was Priam's eldest son and young Paris's brother. He was the general-in-chief of the Trojan armies and was thus the counterpart of Agamemnon, who was in charge of the Greek armies.

During the siege of Troy, he killed Patroclus, whom he had mistaken for Achilles. When Achilles returned to battle, he killed the prince to avenge his friend. After attaching Hector's corpse to his chariot, he rode it along the walls of Troy to display it, then led it back to the Achaean camp, where Priam came to claim it.

He was a paragon of virtue and was celebrated as a gallant prince throughout Antiquity as well as in Medieval literature. His reputation undoubtedly makes him the true hero of the Trojan War, even above Achilles.

Paris, prince of Troy

Paris, named Alexander at birth, was Hector's younger brother. When Hecuba was about to give birth to him, a morbid prophesy was made to her: her child would cause Troy's downfall. Terrified, Priam abandoned him on Mount Ida, where he was rescued by shepherds who renamed him Paris. As an adult, he became known and became the prince of Troy. It was due to him and his desire to kidnap Helen that the war broke out. During the capture of Troy, he killed Achilles before dying himself at the arrows of Philoctetes.

His brother's opposite, he is portrayed in mythology in a less than flattering light – as a womaniser and a coward.

THE TROJAN WAR

THE ACHAEANS' COALITION

Following Helen's kidnapping, Menelaus, the king of Sparta, went to his brother Agamemnon to ask for his help. As he did not have the necessary troops to launch a campaign against the Trojans alone, he sent his counsellor Nestor on a mission around the cities of Greece to remind those concerned about the promise they had made to Tyndareus. In view of Helen's kidnapping, each of them was forced to gather their troops and lend their support to her husband, Menelaus. Nestor travelled across the Peloponnese, Attica, the islands in the Aegean Sea and even went as far as Crete, to King Idomeneus. While all the Greek troops were mobilised, according to Homer the support of two kings in particular was sought: Odysseus and Achilles.

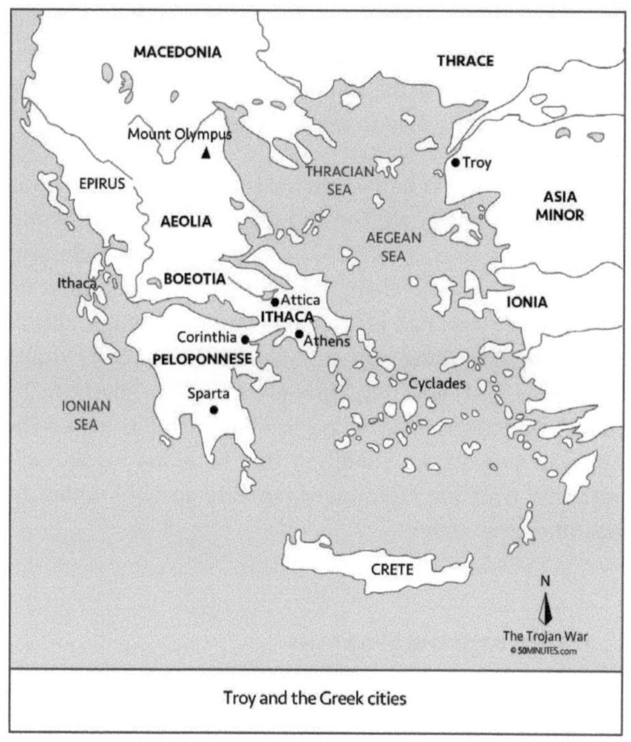

Troy and the Greek cities

The former lived in a small, prosperous kingdom, made up of several well-managed islands. As he had no desire to go to the war that was in the making when he made his oath to Tyndareus, he tried to think of a ruse to get out of it. He decided to feign madness by pretending to plough a field, with both a cow and a horse yoked, and by sowing salt grains while on the move. But his friend Palamedus did not fall for it: he placed Telemachus, Odysseus's young son, in front of the plough, believing that the mad king would not risk running down his own son. He was right: Odysseus immediately halted the animals. He had been discovered and, consequently, had to join the coalition.

As the seer Calchas had predicted that Troy would only fall with Achilles' help, Nestor and Odysseus, who were now rallied to the cause, went to the king of the Myrmidons to convince him to join them. His mother, who did not want him to go to war, had hidden him with Lycomedes, king of Skyros, by disguising him as a girl so that nobody would be able to find him. But, through a ploy by Odysseus, he too was discovered. After negotiating, Achilles joined the Achaean side on the condition that he alone would have authority over the Myrmidons, an elite army of whom he was the commander.

SPARTA AND THE SPARTANS

During the Greco-Persian Wars (5th century BC) and the Peloponnesian War (431-404 BC), Sparta was considered to be a dominant, fearsome military power, and this was the case until the Classical era (510-323 BC), a period during which it refused to join the campaign of Alexander the Great (king of Macedonia, 356-323 BC).

Every citizen aged between 20 and 60 could join the ranks of the hoplites, as long as they were fully dedicated to the role, to the exclusion of all other activity. The hoplites were foot soldiers armed with a shield, a lance and a short sword. They were disciplined and used in the field for complex tactical manoeuvres, which earned them a great reputation in Greece. According to Plutarch, they consistently instilled fear into the hearts of their enemies. They were strictly disciplined from childhood, and received a regulated, specific education, whose reputation is still known, centuries later, due to its military strictness.

THE FIRST TWO CAMPAIGNS AGAINST TROY

According to the *Cypria*, a Trojan epic poem that has been attributed to Stasinus (probably 6th century BC), the fleet assembled by the Achaeans during the two years following Helen's kidnapping landed in Mysia, north of Troy, near the Propontis (modern-day Sea of Marmara). This invasion of Mysia roused the anger of its king, Telephus, who sent his own troops to them. However, overwhelmed by the size of the enemy fleet, he soon surrendered. The Achaeans, despite having suffered some losses, set off towards the West. The war was broken off for eight years.

After this first attempt, the Achaeans gathered a second fleet, this time at Aulis, in Boeotia, near Thebes. However, the anger of the gods prevented Agamemnon's ships from advancing. The seer, Calchas, then made his prophesy: the gods would oppose the Greeks' campaign until Agamemnon had sacrificed his most precious possession, his daughter Iphigenia. The terrible sacrifice was thus made, or narrowly avoided according to some versions of the myth. The ships were released and made their way towards Asia Minor. This second campaign would lead the Achaeans to the shores of Troy, where they met Cycnus, king of Colonae, who was reputed to be invincible. However, Achilles killed him by strangling him with the strap of his helmet, according to most texts.

The Sacrifice of Iphigenia, painting by Charles de La Fosse, 1680.

Troy's high walls, however, were still an impenetrable defence, and the Trojan army stayed hidden behind them as a precaution. Menelaus and Odysseus went there on a diplomatic mission to rescue Helen, but the diplomatic path failed. Achilles then decided to pillage the surrounding land, reducing the Anatolian coasts, which paid a tribute to Troy, to ash.

THE WRATH OF ACHILLES

During the siege of Lyrnessus, Apollo's temple was pillaged and its priestesses taken as slaves: Agamemnon received Chryseis as part of the bounty, while Achilles won Briseis, and fell in love with her. Forced by the gods to return Chryseis to her father, Agamemnon then took Briseis for himself. Achilles, who was deeply offended, became very angry. He withdrew into his tent and decided not to return to battle on the Achaeans' side under any pretext. Subsequently, every time Priam's army went to battle, led by his son Hector, the Achaeans were defeated. Worse still, they were driven back towards the shores and their ships were nearly burned by the Trojan army. Odysseus then made a last attempt to convince Achilles to take up arms once more, as his men were essential for supporting the demoralised Achaeans.

However, it was Patroclus who was eventually responsible for Achilles' return to the battlefield. The young man was restless with impatience at the idea of fighting and donned Achilles' weaponry, according to some texts, and led the Myrmidons to battle. The Achaeans recognised Achilles' armour and returned to battle galvanised. During the battle, Hector, the prince of Troy, thought he had recognised

Achilles and killed him. He soon discovered the truth: it was not Achilles that he had killed, but Patroclus. His body was brought back to the camp and handed to Achilles. He wanted revenge, left his tent and went to battle. He ended up in a one-on-one fight with Hector atop the walls of Troy. After a fierce battle between the two heroes, Achilles killed the Trojan prince. To further satisfy his thirst for revenge, he attached Hector's body to his chariot and paraded it along the ramparts of Troy. Then, taking it back to the Achaean camp, he paraded it again, this time around Patroclus's dead body.

The Funeral Games of Patroclus, painting by Jacque-Louis David, 1779.

The Trojans were horrified at what had happened to their prince, and the gods were offended that a corpse could be treated in this way, in complete violation of all Greek customs. King Priam of Troy went to the enemy camp shortly afterwards to beg for his son's body to be returned, in one of the most moving moments of the Trojan War. Achilles agreed to the request of the old, grieving man: Hector's body was returned to Troy.

THE TROJAN HORSE

The war was now at a stalemate, as neither of the two sides had the necessary troops to win. It was once again Odysseus who, through a subtle ruse, turned the conflict in favour of his own side, even if the idea was given to him by the goddess Athena.

The Achaeans built a large, completely hollow horse out of wood and left it on the shore. They then burned the rest of their camp and boarded their ships, pretending to retreat. In reality, they were carefully hiding their fleet a little further away, near the island of Tenedos, and awaiting the opportune moment to return.

The Trojans celebrated, believing that their high walls had once again protected them from their enemies. When they reached the shore, however, they found an enormous wooden horse and were confused. Why had the Achaeans built it, and why had they abandoned it? Some people thought that it was an offering to the god Poseidon, made to ensure that they would have a peaceful return journey across the Aegean Sea. Others supposed that it was a gift to the goddess Athena. Several people were suspicious: Laocoön urged the Trojans not to trust the Achaeans, believing that the gift must have been tampered with. Despite these differing opinions, the Trojans accepted the gift and began to lead it towards the temple of Athena, located within the city walls. But the horse was huge, and they had to damage the wall to get it into the city. On several occasions, they heard noises coming from inside the horse, but paid no attention to them.

The Procession of the Trojan Horse in Troy, painting by Giovanni Domenico Tiepolo, 1773.

The ruse took effect once night had fallen. Several Achaean warriors, including Odysseus, Menelaus and Neoptolemus, had in fact discreetly hidden themselves inside the horse. Once they were successfully inside the city, on the signal they broke out of the horse and spread out across the city, whose heavy doors they opened. The Achaeans crouched outside could thus enter Troy.

Did you know?

The Achaeans' trick is still famous. Even today we still talk about 'Trojan horses' – in technology for example, where it refers to a seemingly harmless, offensive and often attractive piece of software that in fact carries a malicious programme. This is activated as soon as it is inside the computer, and can sometimes cause significant damage.

THE FALL OF TROY

Troy was then pillaged and ransacked. Fighting broke out across the city, and the Achaeans burned everything in their path. Neoptolemus killed King Priam in his own palace, near the altar of Zeus, as well as Hector's son, Astyanax, before capturing Andromache, who was immediately made a slave. The soothsayer Cassandra, Priam's daughter, hid in the temple of Athena and clung to the goddess's statue to save her life. Ajax dragged her out of the temple and raped her. Spared by Agamemnon, who took her for himself, she later returned to Mycenae with him. Finally, Menelaus killed Deiphobus, one of Priam's sons, and took Helen back.

Achilles was already threatened: his mother had foreseen that he would not return from this campaign alive. His horse Xanthus, who had appeared to him in a dream, had told him that he would die at the hands of a god. Eventually, Paris, with Apollo's support, shot an arrow into Achilles' heel or thigh and killed him. Another source states that it was Polyxena, Priam's daughter, who indirectly killed Achilles: he had fallen in love with her, and on his way to ask Priam for her hand, he was ambushed, and it was Priam who shot him with the fatal arrow.

Death of Achilles, painting by Rubens, 1600.

DID YOU KNOW?

Achilles was the subject of heroic and divine worship for several centuries after his death. Initially contained in Achilleion (Corfu), a town founded on the site where his ashes had been buried, the cult gradually spread throughout continental Greece, as well in various regions along the Aegean Sea, such as in Anatolia or on several islands of the Cyclades.

After the city was ransacked, Agamemnon and Menelaus entered into a dispute: the former wanted to make a sacrifice to the gods, while the latter wanted to return home without delay. Eventually, Menelaus left quickly, eager to return Helen to Sparta. The length of their return voyage, which lasted eight years, was the gods' punishment for having neglected to pay homage to them after their victory.

THE BIRTH OF A NEW MYTH

Achilles was not the only one who had a cult dedicated to him following the Trojan War. Basing his works on the legend of Troy and perpetuating the image of his hero, the Latin poet Virgil (70-19 BC), in the *Aeneid*, recounted the adventures of a young Trojan, Aeneas, who would also gain an impressive reputation. Part of the royal family of Troy through his father, Anchises, and his wife, Creusa, Priam's daughter, Aeneas ardently fought to defend the city and battled valiantly after Hector's death.

During the capture of the city, he fled, grabbing his son, Ascanius, and carrying his father on his back. He was first welcomed in Carthage by Queen Dido, then in Latium (modern-day central Italy) by its king, Latinus, who gave him his daughter Lavinia's hand in marriage. Romulus and Remus, the founding fathers of Rome, were their direct descendants. Ascanius, meanwhile, founded the city of Alba Longa near Rome.

Thus, the Romans found the illustrious roots of their own civilisations in the myth of Troy, and recognised Aeneas as their founding father. Julius Caesar (c. 100-44 BC) even supported his claim to power by insisting that his family descended from the legendary Ascanius, also known as Iulus.

HISTORIOGRAPHY

There are endless sources that tell us the story of the Trojan War, but the quality and time of writing are often very different from one to the next. The *Iliad* and the *Odyssey* are the oldest versions, and even they were written four centuries after the events. Neither of them, however, recount the war from start to finish.

The collection of stories and poems which relate the events that took place in Troy are commonly referred to as epic cycles. They do not form a coherent whole, as there are many contradictions between them. They are complemented by later stories, such as the *Bibliotheca* of Pseudo-Apollodorus from the turn of the millennium, Hyginus's *Fabulae* and Virgil's *Aeneid*, from around the 1st century. Finally, during later Antiquity and throughout the Middle Ages, epic tales, such as *The Sack of Troy* by Tryphiodorus, reinforced a tradition of defining the story of the Trojan War as we know it today.

TROY AND ARCHAEOLOGY

The imprints revealed by archaeology and the work undertaken by Heinrich Schliemann (German archaeologist, 1822-1890) in 1871, then by Ernst Pernicka (Austrian scientist, born in 1950) after 2005 confirmed that nine ancient towns have been built on the site that was formerly occupied by Troy, south of the Dardanelles, in modern-day Turkey. There is proof of human civilisation on the site dating back to the early 2nd millennium BC. The grain-producing plains and cattle-rearing made it a prosperous, commercial and attractive city.

In around 1275 BC, the city was destroyed by an earthquake, but soon rebuilt. The imprints observed on the site have allowed historians to determine that the last phase of inhabitation dates from between 1230 and 1180 BC, before the area was completely abandoned. Archaeology has thus enabled us to corroborate stories from Antiquity that describe Troy as a powerful city with an imposing defensive wall. The city's fate has reached our ears across the centuries, transformed and transfigured through the prism of epic narrative.

SUMMARY

- A myth recounted by numerous epic poems, with Homer's *Iliad* as a key reference point, the Trojan War, which lasted ten years, was fought between the Achaeans and the Trojans.
- The war was declared following the kidnapping of Helen, Menelaus's wife, by Paris, during a visit to Sparta.
- The king of Sparta wanted to avenge this outrageous crime and reminded all the kings of the Greek cities of the promise of Tyndareus, which linked them. This obliged them to come to the aid of Helen's husband in the event that she was kidnapped. A considerable fleet, composed of all the Achaean troops, was thus assembled by Agamemnon, king of Mycenae and Menelaus's brother.
- The Achaeans led two campaigns against Troy. Achilles, a fearsome warrior and invincible demigod, was the key to the Greeks' victory. After withdrawing from combat, he returned to the battlefield to avenge the death of his friend Patroclus and killed Hector, prince of Troy and leader of the Trojan army.
- However, the Trojans were still protected by their city walls. Odysseus then had the idea of building a wooden horse in which the Achaean warriors hid. It was then brought into the city. Following this ruse, Troy was captured and ransacked.
- During the war, Priam was assassinated and his children were killed. Achilles was mortally wounded in the heel by one of Paris's arrows. The young Aeneas fled, keeping alive the hope of rebuilding Troy, and moved to the king-

dom of Latium. This was where his descendants, Romulus and Remus, would later found the powerful city of Rome.

- 31 -

We want to hear from you!
Leave a comment on your online library
and share your favourite books on social media!

FIND OUT MORE

BIBLIOGRAPHY

- Apollodorus (1997) *The Library of Greek Mythology.* Trans. Hard, R. New York: Oxford University Press.
- Homer (2003) *The Iliad.* Trans. Rieu, E. V. London: Penguin Books.
- Homer (2003) *The Odyssey.* Trans. Rieu, E. V. London: Penguin Books.
- Mossé, C. (2004) La Guerre de Troie a-t-elle eu lieu ?. *L'Histoire,* vol.104. [Online]. [Accessed 10 April 2017]. Available from: <http://www.lhistoire.fr/la-guerre-de-troie-t-elle-eu-lieu>
- Vernant, J.-P. (1999) *L'Univers, les dieux, les hommes : récits grecs des origines.* Paris: Seuil.
- Virgil (2003) *The Aeneid.* Trans. West, D. London: Penguin Books.

ADDITIONAL SOURCES

- Koehler, S. B. (2016) *Greek Mythology: Gods, Goddesses, Ancient Myths, Legends and the Stories that Changed Western Civilization.* South Carolina: CreateSpace.
- Scott, A. (2017) *The Mythology of the Trojan War: The History and Legacy of the Mythical Legends about the Battle for Troy.* Cambridge: Charles River Editors.
- Wood, M. (2005) *In Search of the Trojan War.* London: BBC Books.

50MINUTES.com
History
Business
Coaching
Book Review
Health & Wellbeing
ISHIKAWA DIAGRAM
Anticipate and solve problems within your business
Material Method Machine
Mother Nature Measure Men
THE BATTLE OF AUSTERLITZ
NETWORKING
IMPROVE YOUR GENERAL KNOWLEDGE
IN A BLINK OF AN EYE !
www.50minutes.com